Watcher of the Skies

Poems about Space and Aliens

Watcher of the Skies

POEMS ABOUT SPACE AND ALIENS

Edited by Rachel Piercey and Emma Wright

With poems from Sohini Basak, John Canfield, Mary Anne Clark, Mandy Coe, Rebecca Colby, Dom Conlon, Dharmavadana, Julie Anna Douglas, Sarah Doyle, Inua Ellams, David Harmer, Philip Monks, Cheryl Moskowitz, Dale Neal, Rachael M Nicholas, Richard O'Brien, Suzanne Olivante, Abigail Parry, Rachel Piercey, Gita Ralleigh, Robert Schechter, Lawrence Schimel, Mike Sims, Camellia Stafford, Jon Stone, Kate Wakeling, Rob Walton and Kate Wise

Illustrated by Emma Wright

With notes from Rachel Cochrane (Institute for Astronomy, University of Edinburgh)

THE EMMA PRESS
CHILDREN'S BOOKS

ACKNOWLEDGEMENTS

'Uranus: Roll Up, Roll Up', by Sarah Doyle, first published in *Dreaming Spheres: Poems of the Solar System* (PS Publishing, 2014).

'The Alien Restaurant', by David Harmer, first published in *It Came From Outer Space* by Paul Cookson and David Harmer (Macmillan Children's Books, 2013).

'Many Moons Ago', by Lawrence Schimel, first published in *Isaac Asimov's Science Fiction Magazine* in 1997.

THE EMMA PRESS

First published in Great Britain in 2016
by the Emma Press Ltd

ISBN 978-1-910139-43-1

A CIP catalogue record of this book is available from the British Library.

theemmapress.com
queries@theemmapress.com
Birmingham, UK

Contents

WATCHER OF THE SKIES BONUS BITS

Introduction

Thinking about space makes me truly understand the phrase 'mind-blowing'. When I try to get my head around the distances, ages and sizes involved, my brain starts to fizz, bubble and sometimes pop. The light we can see from the galaxy Andromeda has been travelling for 2.5 million years to reach us! You could fit more than a billion of our Suns into the star Mu Cephei! All of this makes me want to write a poem, to try and capture that almost-overwhelming feeling of wonder – and it seems I'm not alone, because all the poets in this anthology have written poems full of awe and adventure, inspired by the possibilities of space.

Poets like to question things. They deal in wonder, fear and excitement; they are interested in both drama and serenity. They love to say 'what if?' and 'imagine this!' and invent characters to live in their made-up worlds. They also like fascinating facts. So it's not really surprising that the subject of space – filled with fireballs, black holes, vivid colours, swirling movement, potential alien life, unanswered questions and vast stretches of noooothing – turns out to be perfect for poets. In fact, the book's title is based on a poem by the nineteenth-century poet John Keats, where he compares reading the translated poems of Homer to the thrill of discovering a new planet: "Then felt I like some watcher of the skies/ When a new planet swims into his ken" ('On First Looking into Chapman's Homer'; 'ken' means knowledge).

Some of our poets blasted off into imaginative worlds and some wrote about the real world of space exploration. We also asked space scientist Rachel Cochrane to write notes for us, to shine a light on the amazing facts behind and within the poems. And everything is marvellously mind-boggling: space is a place where fact and fiction are equally strange and magical. We hope that you will be inspired to write your own space and aliens poems, too: if you look on page 104 you'll find some ideas to get you started.

In fact, it's wonderfully easy to find inspiration to write about space. There are plenty of places where you can look up exciting space research, such as the European Space Agency (ESA) and the National Aeronautics and Space Administration (NASA). The BBC Space website also has lots of amazing facts and some wild, fiery photos of star clusters, galaxies and supernovae. But you can also step outside and see these wonders for yourself. Let your eyes get used to the darkness (it takes several minutes) and look up into the night sky. That's years-old light that is pouring into your eyes! Keep looking... you'll find that more and more layers of stars are revealed, as your eyes adjust. If you are in a very dark area, you might be able to see the pale splash of the Milky Way. And when you make out the figure of Orion, you are standing in the shoes of the Ancient Greeks, who named the constellation after the myth of the gigantic hunter.

I love the names we use for space. Orion, Betelgeuse, evening star, morning star, Milky Way, Cassiopeia, nebulae, red giant, supernova... Aren't they the most gorgeous words? And there are so many intriguing stories behind the constellations. Scorpius is never seen in the sky at the same time as Orion, and one myth tells us that this is because the goddess Gaia tried to kill Orion with a scorpion, after he threatened to get rid of every animal on the planet. Space connects us with human history as well as the history of rock, gas and fire.

Humans have been fascinated by space – and the possibility of extra-terrestrial life – for thousands of years. Cave paintings from over 16,000 years ago show maps of the stars. The Ancient Egyptians kept star charts and the Babylonians kept star catalogues. Roman poet Lucretius mused on the possibilities of other worlds, and sixteenth-century Italian philosopher Giordano Bruno proposed that stars were distant suns with their own planets, which might be able to support life. Just considering the last fifty years, think about all the films, TV shows, books and comics about space travel and specifically aliens. We can't get enough of them! Perhaps it is that they are an unknown quantity, and so we can fill in the gaps for ourselves with qualities which intrigue or scare us. What do you picture when you imagine an alien? Do you think you've been influenced by other people's imaginations?

Space is mind-blowingly enormous. The poets in this book have written about a wonderfully wide spread of themes, but there is infinite room for you to add your own contribution. We hope that *Watcher of the Skies* encourages you to wonder, investigate and invent your own stories about space. Enjoy!

Rachel Piercey
London
September 2016

Watcher of the Skies

How to Brush Your Teeth in Space

Sohini Basak

Far away from home,
the astronauts are measuring meteors
from inside a space station.

Far away from home,
but nearer to some other planets and galaxies,
the astronauts are floating about

in zero gravity, observing stars,
but they are also eating and moving
and sleeping and sometimes maybe farting.

Far away from home,
the astronauts are waking up like us,
and brushing their teeth –

but wait, is there a sink in space?
There is no sink in space,
and no pipes inside the space station,

no tap and no running water.
The astronauts drink out of little pouches
and they even recycle their pee,

but how do they brush their teeth in space?
Because food still gets stuck
between their teeth, there still is morning breath

and it would be a shame
if an alien dropped by but didn't talk for long
because of bad breath,

or worse, when the astronauts
were calculating the speed of a comet
about to hit the earth,

they got distracted by a toothache!
There are probably no dentists
in space either, so the astronauts

must brush their teeth at least twice a day.
And this is how they do it:
they float around and grab

a floating toothbrush,
stick on a little toothpaste from
a floating tube and they brush their teeth

just like you and me, upwards
and downwards, getting the ones
at the back as well, and then they use

those little pouches of water to rinse the foam
and then because there is no sink in space,
or taps, or pipes –

they just swallow it. A little eewww,
but they are astronauts
and they are really really far away from home.

ꕥ

Sohini was inspired to write this poem by astronaut **Chris Hadfield**'s video from the International Space Station. You can watch it here: youtu.be/3bCoGC532p8

Comet

Kate Wakeling

(To be read as quickly as possible, in as few breaths as you can manage.)

I'm a spinning, winning, tripping, zipping, super-sonic ice queen:
see my moon zoom, clock my rocket, watch me splutter tricksy space-steam.

I'm the dust bomb, I'm the freeze sneeze, I'm the top galactic jockey
made (they think) of gas and ice and mystery bits of something rocky.

Oh I sting a sherbet orbit, running rings round star or planet;
should I shoot too near the sun, my tail hots up: *ouch* – *OUCH* – *please fan it!*

And I'm told I hold the answer to the galaxy's top question:
that my middle's made of history (no surprise I've indigestion)

but for now I sprint and skid and whisk and bolt and belt and bomb it;
I'm that hell-for-leather, lunging, plunging, helter-skelter COMET.

ઌ

The origins of the word 'comet' lie in the ancient Greek word for 'long-haired': κομήτης (pronounced 'com-ey-tays'). Can you think why this might be? *You can read about a comet from the Kuiper Belt on page 35.*

Comets are thought to come from two main places in our Solar System: the **Oort Cloud**, a halo of comets around 50,000 times further away from Earth than the Sun, and the **Kuiper Belt**, which lies beyond Neptune.

Stars? Dust? Us?

Inua Ellams

The clever ones say
zillions of days, billions of weeks,
millions of years ago,
stars e x p l o d e d
into f i e r y
clumps
of dust
that cooled
down to sea,
stone, soil,
to human beings,
and I am made of stars.

Everything we are is everything they were.
Everything they were is everything we are.

So were stars made of me?
of denim jeans,
dark chocolate,
pressed flowers,
HOT sauce,
waffles,
football,
t a d p o l e s
and t m l e
u b s
millions of years ago,
zillions of days, billions of weeks,
were stars also scared of darkness what do
the clever ones say?

Art 101 for Aliens

Rebecca Colby

Choose a concentric design,
then measure how it will align.
You must plan out and plot
every spiral and dot,
and ensure that the circles entwine.

Now here's the laborious part:
survey maps before you depart.
Then decide where to rest –
near a henge might be best,
in a field you can fill with your art.

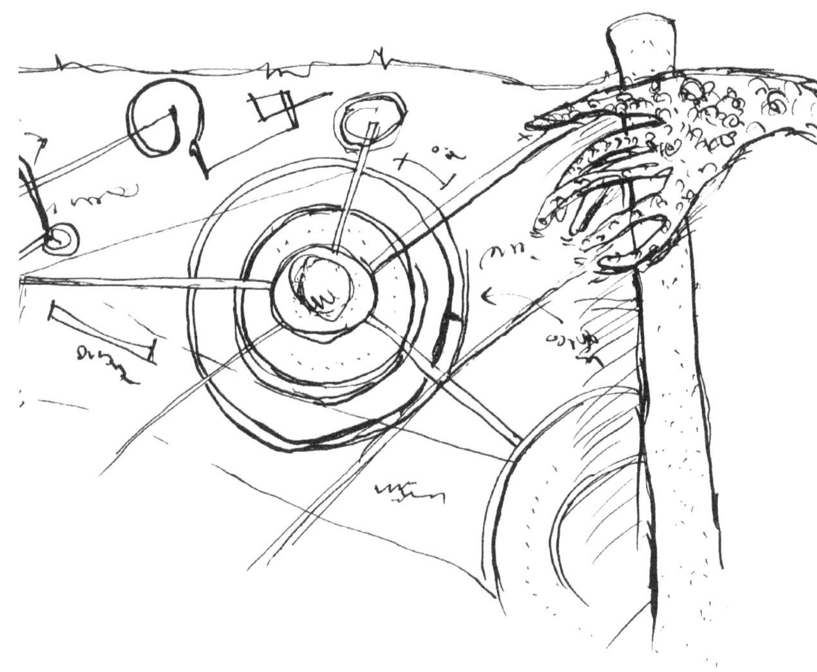

Pack lightly for your Earthbound trip;
all you need for a tool is your ship.
Press the crops down and crush
every grass, reed or rush
on your canvas the ship's landing strip.

The grade for your art will be founded
on how well you've perplexed and astounded
each one of the natives.
So please be creative
and leave them amazed and confounded!

But how big is the universe?

Rachael M Nicholas

It's the big, bigger, biggest.
Bigger even than BIG can describe.

As big as everyone
plus everything
plus the stars
plus the planets
plus all the bits in between
and the in-between bits
where there aren't any bits.

It's the big, bigger, biggest.

Bigger than all the numbers
and all the sounds
and all the light
and all the dark, too.
As big as all that.
And bigger.

If you're still wondering how big the Universe is, have a look at the poem on page 31.

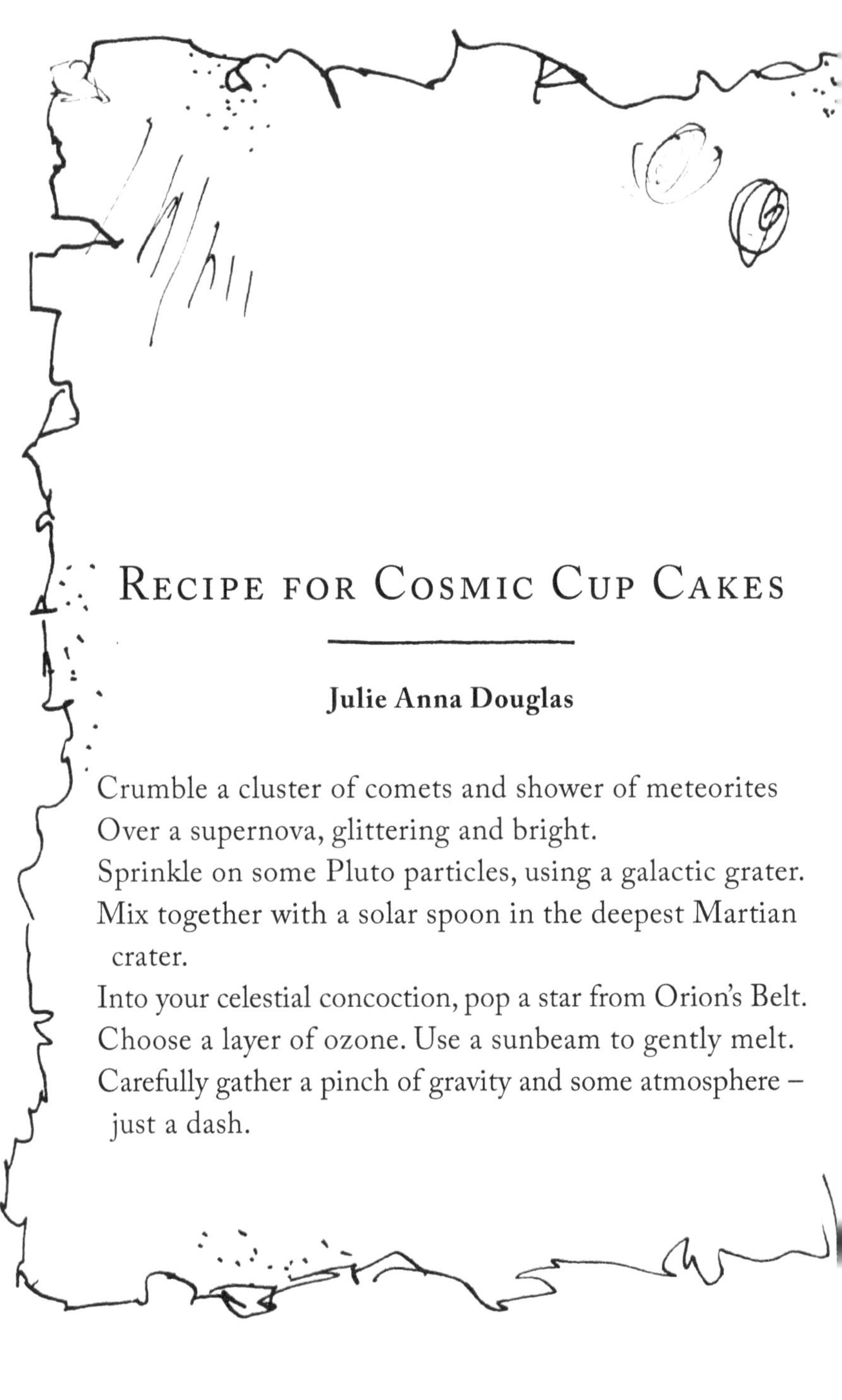

Recipe for Cosmic Cup Cakes

Julie Anna Douglas

Crumble a cluster of comets and shower of meteorites
Over a supernova, glittering and bright.
Sprinkle on some Pluto particles, using a galactic grater.
Mix together with a solar spoon in the deepest Martian
  crater.
Into your celestial concoction, pop a star from Orion's Belt.
Choose a layer of ozone. Use a sunbeam to gently melt.
Carefully gather a pinch of gravity and some atmosphere –
  just a dash.

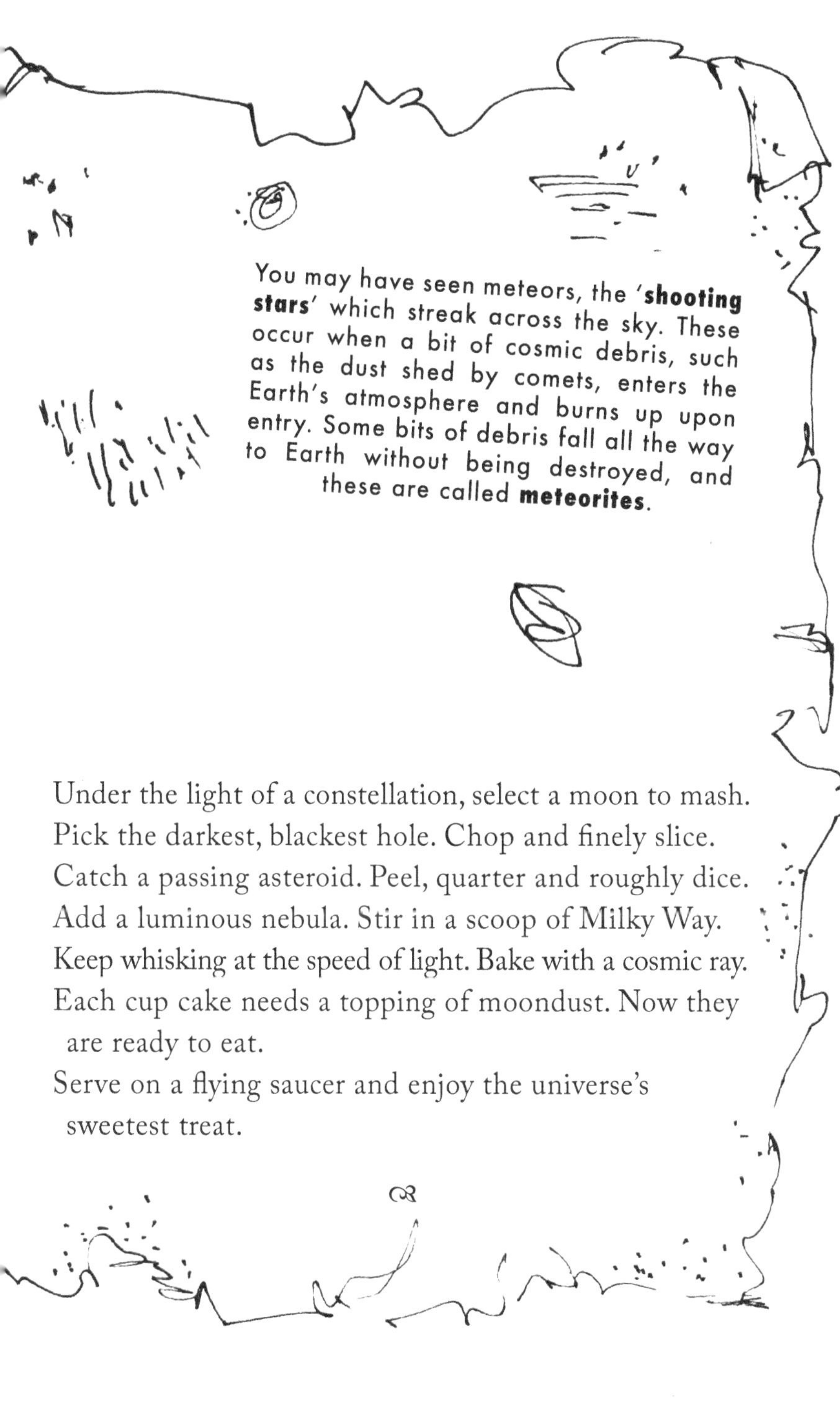

You may have seen meteors, the '**shooting stars**' which streak across the sky. These occur when a bit of cosmic debris, such as the dust shed by comets, enters the Earth's atmosphere and burns up upon entry. Some bits of debris fall all the way to Earth without being destroyed, and these are called **meteorites**.

Under the light of a constellation, select a moon to mash.
Pick the darkest, blackest hole. Chop and finely slice.
Catch a passing asteroid. Peel, quarter and roughly dice.
Add a luminous nebula. Stir in a scoop of Milky Way.
Keep whisking at the speed of light. Bake with a cosmic ray.
Each cup cake needs a topping of moondust. Now they are ready to eat.
Serve on a flying saucer and enjoy the universe's sweetest treat.

Life in the form of bacteria has been discovered in many extreme places, from inside hot sea vents to the dry Atacama desert in Chile. Scientists think that if we find life outside our own planet, it could be similar to these 'extremophile' bacteria.

The **Search for Extraterrestrial Intelligence** (SETI) Institute is an organisation which searches for signals broadcast from alien civilisations using some of the same large telescopes used in many different fields in astronomy, for example in the study of galaxies. They haven't found anyone yet!

Take a trip to an alien restaurant on page 78!

My granddad Burt's an alien

Dale Neal

My granddad Burt's an alien,
he came from outer space
with a dodgy hip in a rocket ship
to save the human race.

His skin's as green as a green string bean
with shades of mushy pea,
and his beard is grey
as is the way for an OAP ET.

His arms protrude like Super Noodles,
long and thin and wobbly;
I hesitate to state which flavour
(ham and mushroom prob'ly).

He wears a cap and a jet pack mac
with boots and baggy kecks,
and says he gets his x-ray specs
from Boots on Planet X.

He's highly wise, advising guys
on how to help mankind.
He's more astute than Doctors Who,
Where, When and Why combined.

He knocks the socks off Brian Cox,
makes Mister Spock look tame:
you'll never find a finer mind
behind a Zimmer frame.

Some days he beams me up from school
aboard his flying saucer;
my mates all say it's way more cool
than mummy's Vauxhall Corsa.

And so at three we go for tea
in zero gravity;
he seems to be the first ET
to eat a Maccy D.

All the staff take photographs
of granddad's UFO,
when in the queue for a drive-through brew
and Happy Meal to go.

We scoff our fries and off we fly
at twice the speed of light.
He takes a right at a satellite
then tucks me in at night.

He tells me tales of comet trails
and stories from the stars
of robot chums with laser guns
(set to stun) on Mars.

Then once he spies I've closed my eyes,
he knows the day is done
and sets off home to get curtains drawn
at Area 51.

He doesn't care to take the stair lift
when he goes to bed:
his rocket slippers get him quicker
up the stairs instead.

He counts his sheep in hyper sleep
then gets up REALLY early.
My granddad Burt's an alien...
and so's my grandma Shirley.

ଓ

Milky Way Disco

Camellia Stafford

Hello, I'm Mercury! I shimmy closest to the Sun,
spinning around her fastest in the Solar System.

I'm your Venus! Only the moon dazzles more.
Like a huge disco ball, I light up the dance floor.

Rock 'n' roll on the red and rockiest planet, Mars!
My Martian snow's the smoke machine at our discos.

The galaxy's greatest dancer, Jupiter, that's me.
My troupe of many, many moons all bop along with glee.

They call me Saturn! I'm a hula-hoop dance fanatic.
My shimmery rings of pink and grey are kaleidoscopic.

I'm Uranus, a street dancer rolling past the Sun on my side.
My Shakespearean moons, Titania, Ariel et al, along for
the ride.

Neptune here! Furthest from the Sun, I'm an ice ice baby.
Can you see me cha cha in the corner of the Milky Way?

This planet needs no introduction. I'm already yours!
Let's dance among the comets, the zillions of stars.

ও

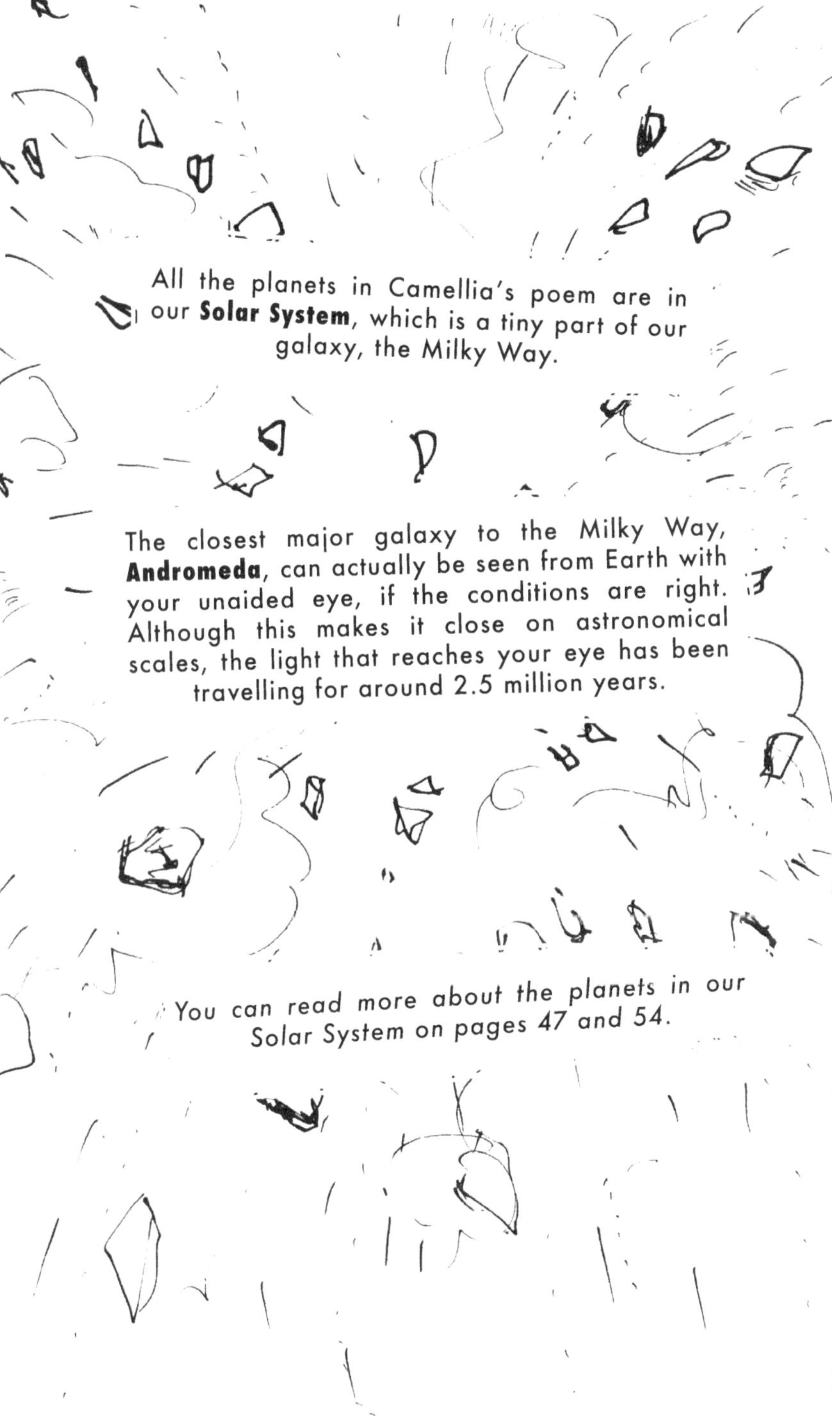

All the planets in Camellia's poem are in our **Solar System**, which is a tiny part of our galaxy, the Milky Way.

The closest major galaxy to the Milky Way, **Andromeda**, can actually be seen from Earth with your unaided eye, if the conditions are right. Although this makes it close on astronomical scales, the light that reaches your eye has been travelling for around 2.5 million years.

You can read more about the planets in our Solar System on pages 47 and 54.

The Starry Messenger

John Canfield

In fifteen hundred and sixty-four
a boy was born, in Italy,
who looked into the skies and saw
things other people could not see:
he saw the universe that spanned
far out beyond our little place,
the air we breathe, the earth we stand
upon, so small in all that space.
He said what no one else would say –
Galileo Galilei.

He stood upon the solid ground
and, looking up into the night,
he thought of planets spinning round
the sun: Copernicus was right,
who said that earth was not the core
for all the planets, and the sun;
they do not spin around us, nor
are we the most important one.
He shocked the world, back in his day –
Galileo Galilei.

He dreamed of looking past what man
had seen using the naked eye;
he formulated his own plan
to look into the bright night sky.
He built himself a telescope
and pointed it into the black,
provoking anger in the Pope,
who made him say he took it back:
too risky seeing things his way –
Galileo Galilei.

But out amongst the planets were
the satellites that proved them wrong:
he watched the moons of Jupiter
spin round, he listened to their song
and wrote down what he saw and heard,
and drew the mountains of the moon;
we see the stars in every word,
and now hear the celestial tune
that one man taught us all to play –
Galileo Galilei.

☙

Galileo Galilei was a professor of mathematics at the University of Padua, Italy, who built one of the first telescopes in 1609. His pioneering observations led him to the dangerous conclusion that the Earth did not lie at the centre of the Universe. Galileo's defence of **heliocentrism** (the idea that the Earth revolves around the Sun – which we now know to be true) eventually led to his arrest.

In 1638, just four years before his death at the age of 77, he attempted the first measurement of the speed of light. Fans of Galileo can visit the museum named after him in Florence; Museo Galileo proudly displays three of his fingers!

COMPARED TO WHAT?

Robert Schechter

A pebble isn't all that big
compared to stones or boulders,
but it's a mountain to the ant
who lifts it on his shoulders.

And if you were a molecule,
an atom or a proton,
a water drop would be a lake
for you to sail your boat on.

An elephant is huge for sure;
its trunk would crush your scale.
And yet it doesn't seem that large
if you're a humpback whale.

I've always claimed the Earth is huge,
and no one has denied it.
And yet the Sun alone could hold
a million Earths inside it.

Then certainly the *Sun* is huge?
Well no, wait just a minute!
The star Mu Cephei could contain
a billion Suns within it!

Can we agree Mu Cephei's huge?
The biggest of Red Giants,
it's dwarfed in size by galaxies!
Believe me! This is science!

The galaxy that it calls home,
our own, the Milky Way,
contains a hundred billion stars.
Mu Cephei's *one*, okay?

And though Mu Cephei dwarfs the Sun,
is bigger and more shiny,
compare it to the Milky Way
and you will think it's tiny.

And so it goes. The Milky Way,
astronomers inform us,
although at first it may appear
mind-bogglingly enormous,

is hardly bigger than a speck,
when all is said and done.
Of billions and billions of galaxies,
the Milky Way's just one.

So when you're asked if something's big,
say, 'I will answer, but…
before I do, please tell me this…
Big? Compared to *what?*'

ଔ

There are billions of galaxies in our Universe, and scientists separate them into two main types: **blue spirals**, which form high quantities of stars, and **red ellipticals**, which aren't forming many stars. The processes which lead to 'galaxy death' – where a galaxy transforms from blue to red – are hotly debated in astronomy.

Message for Rosetta

Rachel Piercey

Rosetta, Rosetta,
tell us how long it
will take you to get to
the Kuiper-belt comet?

Ten years, ten years,
past asteroids, Mars,
soaking up sun rays
to power my task.

Rosetta, Rosetta,
what's in your pocket
to give as a gift
to the Kuiper-belt comet?

A message, a message,
a disc etched with words,
so whoever finds it
might understand Earth.

Rosetta, Rosetta,
now you're in orbit!
What have you found
on the Kuiper-belt comet?

It's singing, it's singing,
a high flinty hum –
don't know what it means
but our talk has begun…

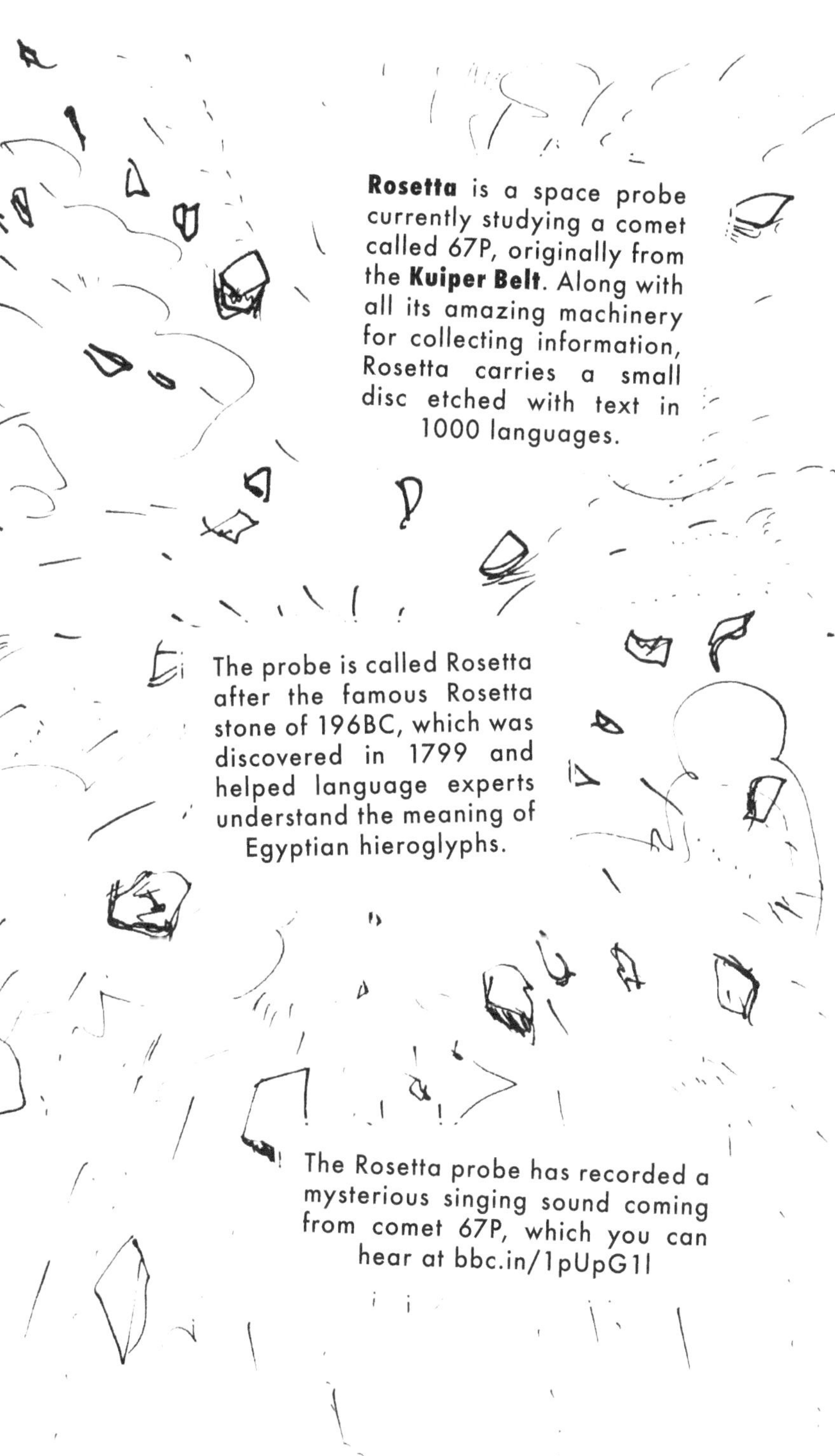

Rosetta is a space probe currently studying a comet called 67P, originally from the **Kuiper Belt**. Along with all its amazing machinery for collecting information, Rosetta carries a small disc etched with text in 1000 languages.

The probe is called Rosetta after the famous Rosetta stone of 196BC, which was discovered in 1799 and helped language experts understand the meaning of Egyptian hieroglyphs.

The Rosetta probe has recorded a mysterious singing sound coming from comet 67P, which you can hear at bbc.in/1pUpG1l

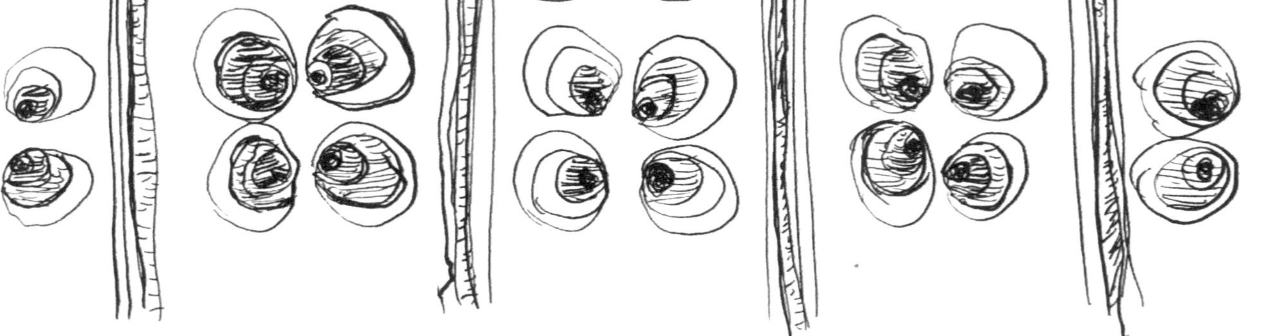

High Frontier

Richard O'Brien

Listen: it's the 1970s. My granddad's wearing flares,
and a nasty shade of burgundy is carpeting the stairs,
and there's rubbish in the streets and there's pollution in the air,
but it's all OK: we'll build a home in space.

Yes, it's been suggested once or twice; never quite like this, though.
Where we'll go the gravity's so low you couldn't hold a disco:
if you jumped in astral Hull you'd land in space's San Francisco,
and the eyeliner would slide right off your face.

See, we're going to an area that's called Lagrange Point Five,
which is held in perfect equilibrium on either side:
it's the still point at the centre of the cosmic shuck and jive,
and it's where our brave new settlement will float.

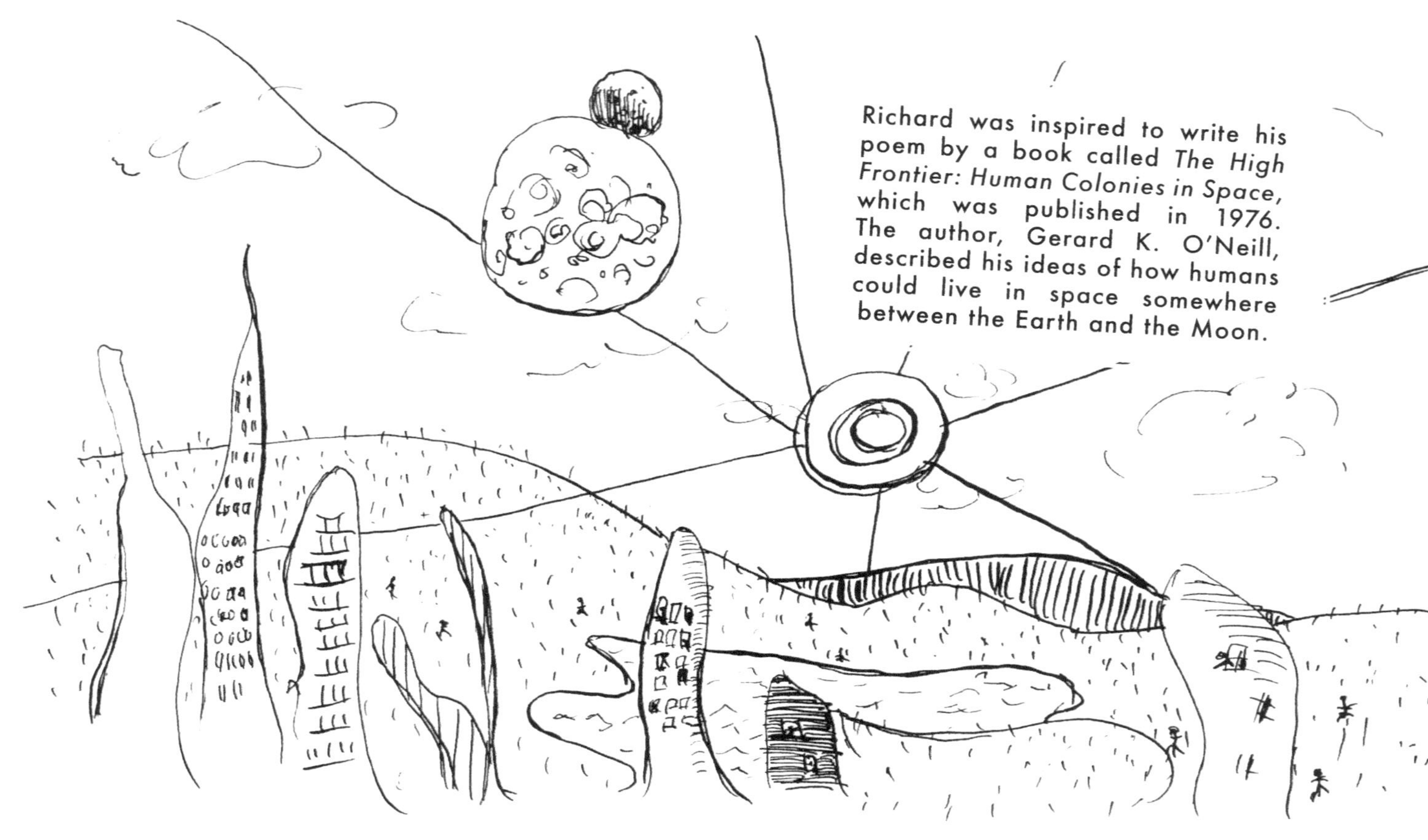

Richard was inspired to write his poem by a book called *The High Frontier: Human Colonies in Space*, which was published in 1976. The author, Gerard K. O'Neill, described his ideas of how humans could live in space somewhere between the Earth and the Moon.

It will be a giant tube rotating slowly round a centre,
and a colony the size of modern Ludlow will be sent there,
but there'll be no Tudor buildings and there'll be no Marks & Spencer:
there'll be oxygen in tanks, and dogs can vote.

We'll incorporate a river and a glade and a lagoon,
and the site will be convenient for mining on the moon –
we're expecting to be sending in our planning permits soon,
and we'll build a Tuscan hill town in the stars.

This is called the High Frontier, but it's well within our reach,
since we're nothing if not conquerors: *Once more unto the breach!*
We'll have mansions and marshmallows there, hold parties on the beach,
and we'll wonder if they have nightlife on Mars.

And by now you're surely asking: can we go there after class?
But I'm sorry to inform you that this never came to pass:
what you know on Earth as Astroturf is not galactic grass,
and we didn't launch our spinning disc of dreams.

There are lots of great ideas that don't make it beyond talk
(like thought-activated back-scratchers, the knife part of a spork,
an injection against boredom) – but we need to walk the walk
if we want to swim in interstellar streams.

So it's not the 1970s, and shoes are normal height,
and we've got a world in front of us where lots of things aren't right,
and our planet's problems seem to be more pressing than space flight –
but you know, you'll never know if you don't go.

So if I were you, I'd take those flares and glitter off the shelf
and consider what the universe is offering: a wealth
of great wonders. And why shouldn't you discover them yourself?
Well, you know, if you don't go you'll never know.

ᴓ

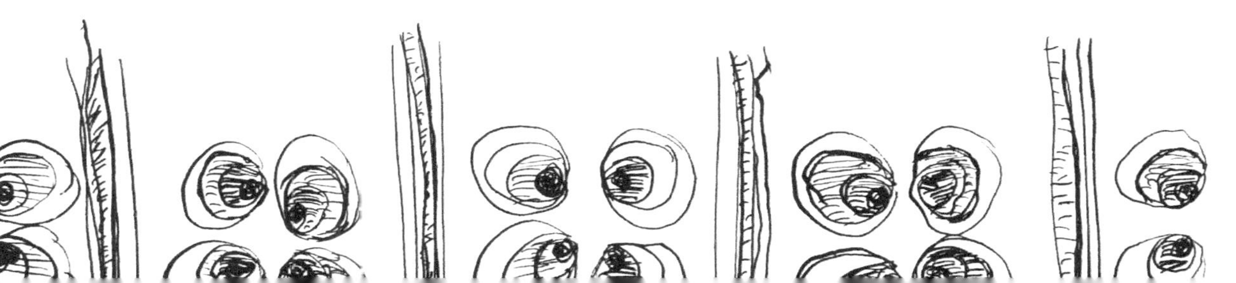

A Dog in Space

Mary Anne Clark

Far away, far away,
I think perhaps there's a dog up there
for me, *my* dog.
A Russian space dog that history forgot?
Laika, Mushka, Veterok,
Belka, Strelka, Ugolyok,
then *my* dog, eternally
orbiting the world, just out of my reach
but always circling, always there.

Perhaps it can see me from its swirling capsule?
My dog barks when I am laughing;
my dog howls when I am crying.
So I know that's my own dog,
though I'll never have a dog on Earth.

Light years, light years
separate me and my astronaut dog –
but in the stars that glint like dew on a rose
I see the shine on my dog's wet nose;
its paws tread planets;

it maps new worlds as it steers through space;
rain pours on Earth
when it cocks its leg at the moon's lamp post.
I feel my dog's soft fur in the sun's warm halo
and see it wagging its tail in the flick of the rainbow.

ℬ

In 1957, **Laika** became the first dog to be placed into orbit around the Earth. She and her vessel **Sputnik 2** remain icons of the ambitious Soviet space programme, which later succeeded in sending both the first man, Yuri Gagarin, and the first woman, Valentina Tereshkova, to space.

Although Laika unfortunately didn't make it back to Earth alive, many of the other dogs mentioned here did. The inappropriately-named Smelaya (Смелая), which means 'Brave', completed her mission despite attempting to flee before the launch!

Letters

Rob Walton

Dear Mercurians,
You spend half of your time complaining
about excess heat,
and fifty per cent saying you're too cold.
Please make your minds up.

Dear Venusians,
Perhaps putting your clammy hands in your pockets
and investing in a decent vacuum cleaner
would get rid of some of that bothersome
heat-trapping dust
(and save you having to import
dodgy ice from the Neptunians,
with the accompanying
exorbitant transportation fees).

Dear Humans,
Maybe you should spend
less time watching television
re-runs of The Blue Planet and
more time sorting out your thermostat.

My dear Martians,
Red is *so* last season.

Dear Jovians/Jupiterians,
When you've decided on your name,
how about considering
the old Earth adage that
size isn't everything?

Dear Saturnians,
I'm old enough to remember
some of you playing
with a hoop and stick
and a hula hoop,
so don't think you can
run rings round me
with all of your hoop-la.

Dear Uranians,
What exactly do you intend
to do with all those moons?
The polite and decent thing
would be to share them out.

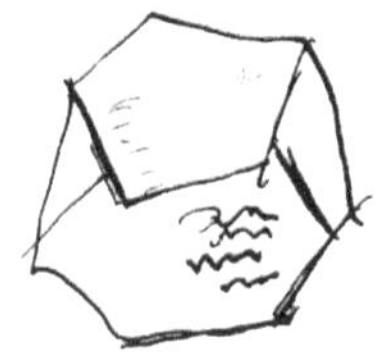

Dear Neptunians,
Have you ever thought
about sorting out
those bright blue clouds?
I mean, you wouldn't want
to be mistaken for Earth.
Would you?

Dear Plutonians,
Your claims were dismissed
a long time ago.
Please leave the system at once.

☙

Many Moons Ago

Lawrence Schimel

At first I liked the Lunar Base.
It was exciting. New. I liked
the thought of living out in space.
But there was nothing to be psyched

about. The moon was dull. It had
no life, besides the Base. Each day,
each week, were all the same. Then Dad
got transferred once again. *Hooray!*

I cried, *We're going someplace new.*
But it was just another Base,
on another moon. Nothing to
do or see, just like the old place.

I miss the planet of my birth,
its summer heat and winter snow.
There was a time we lived on Earth,
but that was many moons ago.

ଓ

The Moon is described as dull compared to Earth because it doesn't have seasons like we do. Seasons on planet Earth come about through a combination of our axis tilt and our atmosphere.

When the Northern Hemisphere is tilted towards the Sun, it's blessed by warm weather, while the Southern Hemisphere suffers through winter. As the Earth orbits the Sun, fortunes change and the Southern Hemisphere enters Spring and Summer. The Moon is about 15 times less strongly tilted than the Earth, so it doesn't experience the same seasonal changes in heat.

The Way Planets Talk

Dom Conlon

What might we hear if we listened
for the star-forged language
the planets used when sound was new
and words had no full stops?

We might hear the distant vowels
of Neptune, each word as long
as life, each sun-abandoned syllable
the sound of a breathing whale.

We might hear the soft lilt of Uranus,
with its dictionary of duck eggs
plopped into blue flour – a thousand
definitions in a single air-thrown sigh.

We might hear the singing voice of Saturn,
with its billion letter alphabet
scattered along a single groove,
its voice recorded in a tantrum of sentences.

We might hear the whirling words of Jupiter,
where ‘hello’ is the oil in an engine
and ‘I love you’ is the red echo
of a candle flame dying at sunrise.

We might once have even heard Mars
utter its own name before the words dried
on the tip of its burnt tongue, before
a final, thirst-silenced cry scratched the dust.

We might hear Venus,
Venus who speaks in a dialect
separated from our own
only by a dream on a too-warm night.

And nestled between stone-fist silences
we might hear Mercury
wailing like a boiled baby
each time the sun scrubs its face.

If we listened we might hear these planets,
and take the language from their molten cores
and learn that distance is a comma,
a pause in how we talk about tomorrow.

☙

Five of the planets in our Solar System are visible from Earth with the naked eye, each named after a different god or goddess by the Romans.

Mercury, a swift-moving planet, was given the name of the god of travel and **Venus**, who shone brightly in the sky, the goddess of love.

Mars, red and bloody, was named after the god of war and **Jupiter**, the largest of all the planets, the chief of the gods. Finally, **Saturn** was named after the god of agriculture.

If **extraterrestrial life** exists, where could we find it? Liquid water is necessary to support life, so we need to search for places at the right temperatures – at low temperatures water freezes, and at high temperatures it boils.

The so-called 'Habitable Zone' or 'Goldilocks Zone' is the region around a star where the temperature is in the range 273K (zero degrees celsius) to 373K (100 degrees celsius).

Alien Boy

Mike Sims

There were three of them then on this trip,
shipping to school in England from India
on a liner bright as Dover cliffs.
The ocean flat night after night
as they ran about the decks,
the moon their searchlight.

When the New Boy removed his hand,
showing them twitching wires at his wrist,
not blood or pus, they gasped, not least
because he was the strongest –
his prowess had made all three of them brave.

And now they looked more carefully,
yes, there was the same gleam through
his slicked-back hair and, when he did the trick,
his transparent skin. They felt more than saw
the blood bubbling in his arteries,
the revolving motors of his eyeballs.

He loved to swim –
plunged like a stone off the side.
But he softened in water, fur-edged like paper,
and afterwards, fungal: thick and lumpy
around his elbows, knees, ears and jaw.
He lacked definition – you might even say flabby.

And they'd never see him come aboard
so imagined him like a spider flipped
high on a wave, cramponing the ship's flank
and leaping feather-light on deck with a grin.
Though an alien – that much was clear –
they wouldn't desert him: he was their friend.

But England worried them –
as if arriving from elsewhere weren't challenge enough!
What might happen there to an alien like him?
Was the sea's dragging swell a dangerous omen?
The strange stars spinning – could he turn the boat?

☙

Up Above

Mandy Coe

What's up above?
asked sparrow of her brother.
    It's the twinkle of song in the nest of black moss.
    There's the Great White Egg, the Wheatfield and
      the Feather.
Have they been there long?
Forever my love, forever.

What's up above?
asked tadpole of his father.
    It's Silver Spawn in the great black pond.
    There's the Lily, the Heron and the Swimming
      Beaver.
Have they been there long?
Forever my love, forever.

What's up above?
asked elephant of his sister.
    It's the kind-eyed herd, in the plains of sleep.
    There's the curve of Tusk, the Trunk and the River.
Have they been there long?
Forever my love, forever.

What's up above?
asked the whale of her mother.
    It's the flash of hooks, the infinite net,
    the glitter of fishes forever asleep.
Have they been there long?
Forever my love, dive deep.

☙

The Algonquin Calendar of Changing Moons

Cheryl Moskowitz

Dark nights growing

Wolf Moon
Snow Moon
Worm Moon

Nobody likes me

Buds start showing

Pink Moon
Flower Moon
Strawberry Moon

Served with cream and a silver spoon

Warm sun glowing

Buck Moon
Sturgeon Moon
Harvest Moon

Last one home's a pumpkin!

Leaves are blowing

Hunter's Moon
Beaver Moon
Cold Moon

When the year ends will you still be my friend?

Love bestowing

My Moon
Your Moon
Blue Moon

Round the earth and back again

ര

The Moon, just like people, can be changeable. It appears to change shape, size and even colour. The Algonquins are indigenous inhabitants of North America who speak the Algonquin language, and they gave a separate name to each full moon that occurs throughout the year so they could use it to keep track of the seasons.

When you look up at the night sky, it's hard to make sense of how far away objects are. A simple way to understand these huge scales is to imagine that the length of your foot is the diameter of the Earth. In 30 footsteps, you could reach the Moon, but it would take over 10 thousand steps (around 5 miles) to reach the Sun.

Poets in Space!

Abigail Parry and Jon Stone

Emily Dickinson in Space

Because I could not stop for Time –
It kindly stopped for me –
My spaceship veered and plunged into
A Singularity.

The Lights went out, the Thrusters too –
The Engine coughed and died –
I felt for my Chronometer –
It had spaghettified –

Since then – Millenniums have passed –
Yet shorter than the Day –
I picked a Fight with Time and Space
And Relativity.

Shakespeare in Space

Shall I compare thee to the Milky Way?
Thou art more restless and disorderly.
A raging ball of gas at least obeys
The laws of thermal flux and entropy.

Tornados tear across the face of Mars,
The lava pits of Venus roil and shriek,
The Sun erupts in white-hot solar flares,
But you – you make a nebula look meek.

Black holes and supernovas tend to sit
In orbits more or less predictable.
But Newton could not brag that you submit
To one scintilla of his Principles.

But ah, my little quark, so charmed and strange,
There's not one atom of you I would change.

What's the **smallest thing in the Universe**? Even smaller than atoms are the protons and neutrons that form their nuclei (central parts). And even smaller than protons and neutrons are **quarks**.

There are six types, or 'flavours' of quark: *up, down, top, bottom, strange* and *charm*. A proton is composed of two 'up' quarks and one 'down' quark, and a neutron is composed of one 'up' quark and two 'down' quarks.

Ted Hughes in Space

Guest-starring Fox McCloud AKA Star Fox

I imagine this midnight moment's starfield:
Something else is blasting
Through the vacuum's loneliness
Past the moonbase where my instruments tick.

Through my telescope I see no comet:
Something more near
With a flamier tail
Is entering the lunasphere.

Hot, hurtlingly as an asteroid,
A combat spaceship rips through dark;
Fine paws serve a moment, that now
And again now, and now, and now

Slips the ship between debris
And satellites, and neon laser fire
Lights up the sky and the cockpit
Where the pilot boldly plots his course

Through systems, his eye
A narrowing deepening greenness,
Brilliantly, pluckily
Striking at an evil empire

Till, with a sudden sharp shot, Star Fox
Is gone again into a hole in space.
The telescope is empty still. The instruments
Have gone crazy.

Ono no Komachi in Space

The colour of this supergiant
Is already dimmed
While in idle drift
My air runs low
As I watch a meteor storm

Lord Byron in Space

So we'll go no more a-moonroving
Across the lunar seas,
Though traffic, and manoeuvring,
And parking are a breeze.

For the Sea of Storms is fraught,
And the Sea of Vapours grim,
And the Lake of Hatred's not
The sort in which I'd swim.

Though the stars be supernova-ing
And the Earth a blue balloon,
Yet we'll go no more a-moonroving –
I've had it with the moon.

☙

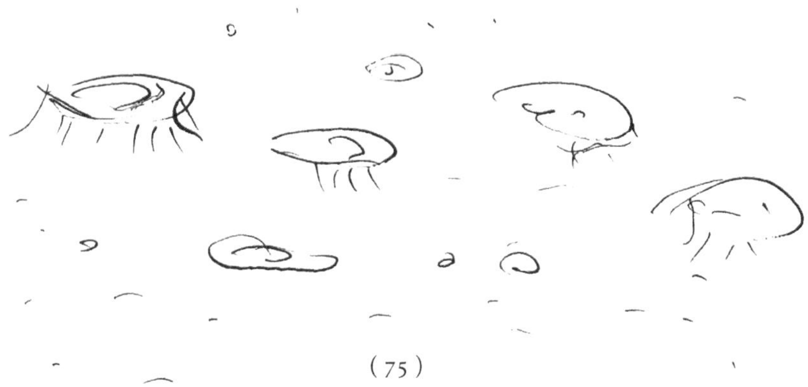

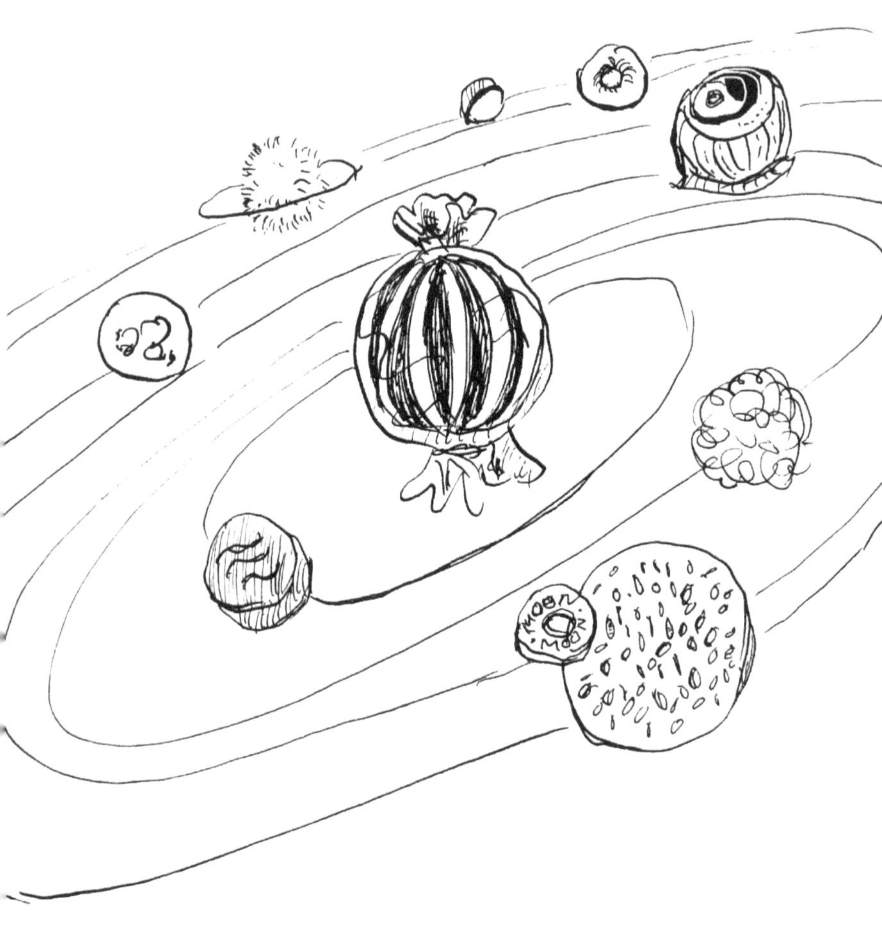

We don't really have any **black holes** in our Solar System – luckily! *You can read more about black holes on page 89.*

Solar System Candy

Gita Ralleigh

If I ate the solar system,
the moon would taste
strange and dusty
as Turkish Delight.
Planets would be
giant gobstoppers,
except Saturn and Jupiter –
those gas giants
fizz like sherbet,
or melt like candy floss
in your mouth.
The meteor belt
pops and crackles
like space dust.
Comets leave a minty sting
on your tonguc.
Black holes taste of cola bottles.
Or memories
you once had
and lost.

The Alien Restaurant

David Harmer

Went down to the alien restaurant
Saw the menu there
Strange and slimy, it said 'Try Me,
Eat Here If You Dare!'

Went down to the alien restaurant
Ate Grooblik-Grotgrunge curry
All wriggle and writhe, still alive
Slurped it in a hurry.

Went down to the alien restaurant
Ate Misty Martian soup
Glowing green in a steamy tureen
Intergalactic gloop.

Went down to the alien restaurant
Ate Venusian Swogglebat pie
Clunky, chewy, sticky and gooey
Hot as the sun in the sky.

Went down to the alien restaurant
Ate Splogglesplat spaghetti
Warm and wormy, really squirmy
I went all red and sweaty.

Went down to the alien restaurant
Ate crispy Gaggle Fly eggs
Lumpy, bumpy, made me jumpy
With shaking, quaking legs.

Went down to the alien restaurant
Ate Feathery Fuddlebird stew
All squeals and squeaks, claws and beaks
Really delicious too.

Went down to the alien restaurant
To eat some Siloobian swan
But in its place was empty space
And that's just where it's gone.

ℭ

Countdown

Philip Monks

10
It's so noisy in here!
That's why I'm shouting!

9
Look at all these flashing lights.
Wonder what they're for?

8
Wish I'd had breakfast.
You should always have breakfast.

7
I think I forgot to feed the hamster.
There's plenty of food in its bowl.

6
Feeling a little bit nervous.
Try not to think about it.

5
I want to go to the toilet.
No you don't.

4
I'm feeling thirsty.
Too late now.

3
Don't want to do it.
Yes, you do.

2
Space is a long way off.
Won't be soon.

1
Blast off!

Up we go.
Feeling heavy.
Up we go.
Feeling very, very heavy.
Up we go.
Wow! I'm as light as a feather.
You're as light as an astronaut.

ଔ

The **gravity** an astronaut experiences isn't actually much weaker than it is on Earth. An astronaut feels weightless because both they and their spacecraft are accelerating under gravity in the same way – just like when your body leaves the seat on a free-falling rollercoaster ride.

Uranus: Roll Up, Roll Up

Sarah Doyle

A tumbling clown,
feet up, face down,
conventions all defied.

Anomalous
but glorious,
suspended on my side.

A lissom cat,
an acrobat,
dispensing with trapeze.

Born to enthral,
skewed juggling ball,
I roll and flip with ease.

A snookered globe,
a norma-phobe,
my axis quite a shock.

I've far more flair
when you compare
those other lumps of rock.

My carbon rings,
most wondrous things,
rotate from north to south.

Will not conform,
reject the norm –
a giant, laughing mouth.

My orbit's range
is deeply strange:
eccentric is the word.

A circle? No,
distorted O,
delightfully absurd.

My wacky streak
is quite unique,
distinguished cosmos-wide.

Exhibiting
what planets bring
to pass, when they collide.

☙

Uranus is the only giant planet whose equator is nearly at right angles to its orbit – imagine it rolling around whilst orbiting the Sun, rather than spinning like the Earth. Scientists can't say definitively why it has this tilt, but it could have been caused by a collision with an Earth-sized object.

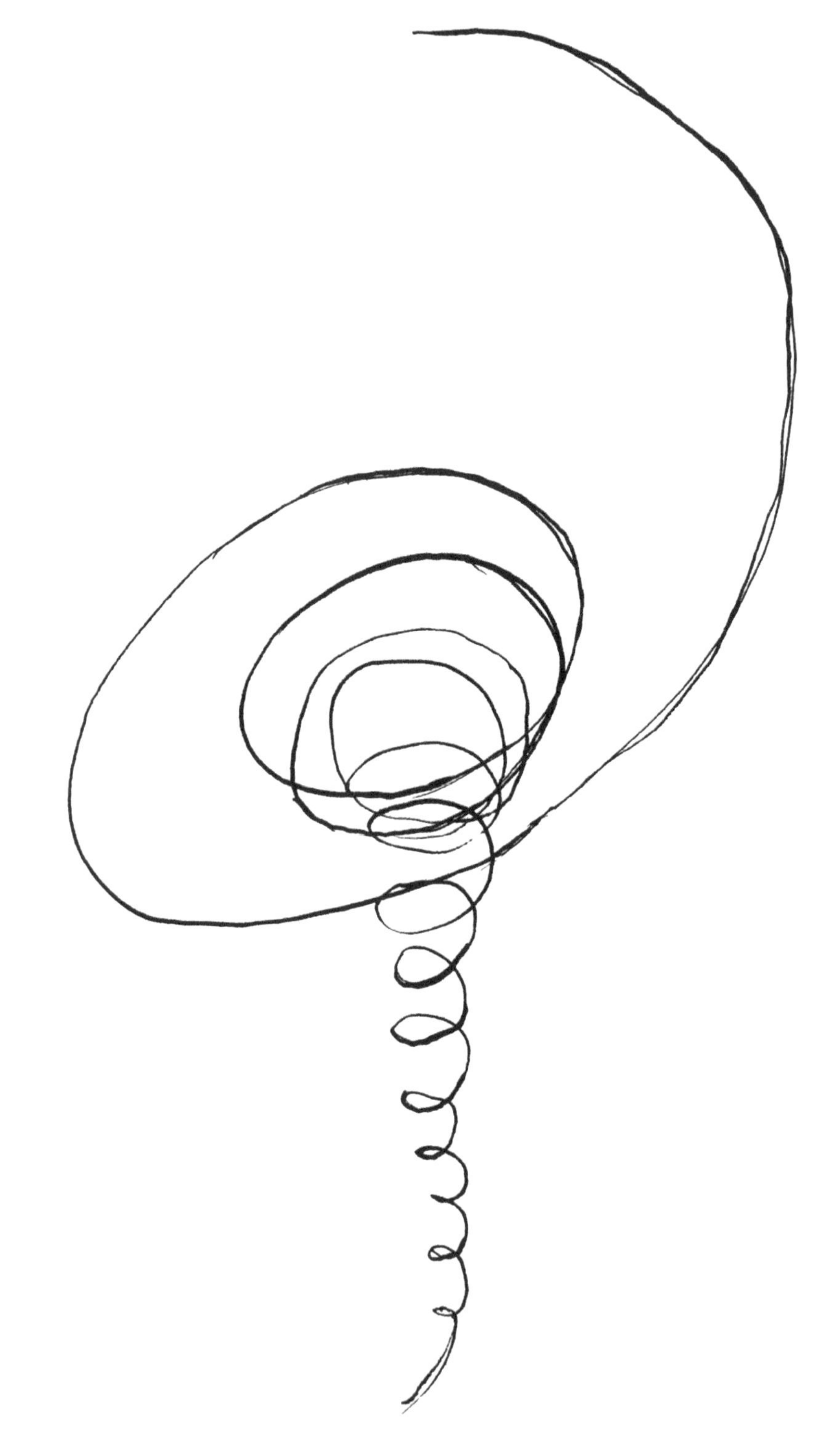

The Hungry Galactic Plug Hole

Suzanne Olivante

star swallower
gas guzzler
gulping garbage feeder

matter muncher
dust digester
cosmic vacuum cleaner

yawning glutton
belly button
centre of the spiral

super suction
dark destruction
great galactic gyral

beyond control
it swallows whole
you can't resist the tug

black hungry hole
the light it stole
please someone find the plug

ଔ

Back in 1783 a little-known scientist and clergyman, John Michell, came up with the idea of 'dark stars', the dense regions found in the centres of galaxies which are now known as **black holes**.

Once light passes a certain point in a black hole – the Schwarzschild radius – it can't escape, so we aren't able to observe black holes directly. However, tell-tale signs of a black hole's presence include the light radiated from **accretion disks** (bands of gas, dust and stellar debris that surround the black hole), and the presence of **powerful jets of particles**.

Stars

Kate Wise

twinkle – right? That's what stars do.
Except…
stars also
glitter glisten glister
stars glimmer
stars shimmer
stars flicker
stars gleam
stars sparkle
stars scream
– hair burning, back-streaming through the skies.

Stars scintillate.
Believe it or not,
some stars 'blinter'; some 'pink'.
Stars roar and hiss and splash and rage and sting;
stars stab and shoot and fly.
Stars BURST!
Stars die...
So, sure, stars twinkle –
for some that's true.
But what will your stars do?

How to get to Zagnaraputta

Dharmavadana

Stand on your head. Whistle the first tune you think of,
divide it by two and whistle it again.
Look the wall right between the eyes and say:
'Mr Elvis P Thrang is not at home.' It should open
  immediately.
You will see what appears to be a spinning pink and blue
  cloud.
Don't be scared. This is the galaxy M83 in the constellation
  Hydra.
Let go soon, or you will miss the entrance.

You're aiming for a complicated swirl
that looks like a bottomless '8' just to the left of the centre.
That mouth with fangs dripping molten iron
and breathing a green plasma – ignore it:
it's a mirage left there by a previous traveller
who dropped it in fear of what he really saw.
When you see what he really saw you'll understand.
Your sunglasses won't help. But you must approach it
  head-on.

Shut your eyes if you need to, but dive straight in.
You may feel certain squidgy sensations
and then a sort of nothingness and a roaring, rushing noise
and then something that no guide book
or instructions can predict, or prepare you for –
but don't worry: you *are* still alive
even though it might not feel like it. Keep going.

Your head will bump up against something like the other side of water.
Take hold of the sides, pull back and go through.
When it feels as if there is nothing below you,
just let yourself go and dive. It may be best to sing as you fly –
your country's national anthem, your favourite pop song
or anything you can think of. You may need a lot of tunes.
The length of this descent varies according to who you are,

the number of letters in your name and your age divided by
the number of planets in your Solar System,
but your landing will be soft.

You will find yourself at the edge of a lake.
Across it is a floating path to three towers in the middle,
each crowned by light that streams in all directions like
the wind.
As you walk, the path will disappear behind you –
and be aware that the lake is infinitely deep
and full of monsters that have been banished from Earth
and are waiting for revenge. But don't worry.
You will hear the songs of the visitors who came before you
and they will make you feel better,
or not. You are approaching Zagnaraputta. There is no
going back.

ଓ

Watcher of the Skies
Bonus Bits

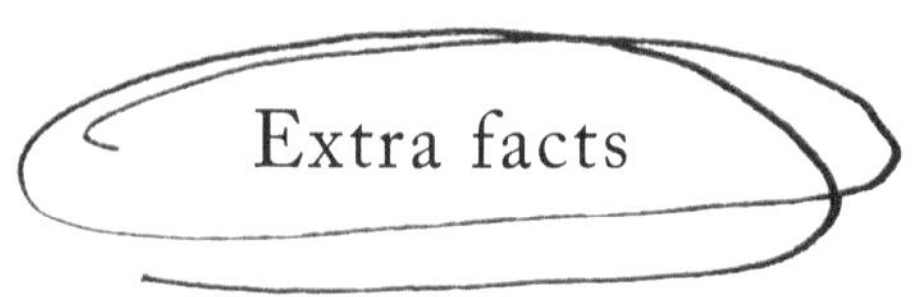

Extra facts

★ Can we measure the size of the Universe?

Consider the lower-pitched noise you hear from a police car's siren as it moves away from you, and the higher pitch as it approaches. A similar effect occurs in astronomy, called 'redshift'.

The light we receive from astronomical objects becomes redder when they are moving away from Earth. Due to the expansion of the Universe, the furthest objects are moving away from us fastest. Measurements of objects' redshifts can tell us how far away they are.

Read Rachael M Nicholas's poem 'But how big is the universe?' on page 12.

☆ Why do stars twinkle?

Stars twinkle, or 'scintillate', because we see them through the turbulent gases surrounding the Earth – that is to say, its atmosphere. Stars are actually so far away that we should see them as motionless points on the sky, but as their light passes through the atmosphere it's bent in different directions.

Many of the telescopes we use to observe stars are built on space stations, because we need to place our cameras above the atmosphere to gain a really sharp image.

Read Kate Wise's poem 'Stars' on page 92.

★ What do we know about galaxy M83, mentioned in 'How to get to Zagnaraputta' (page 95)?

It takes 15 million years for light from galaxy M83 to reach our telescopes on planet Earth, so the pink and blue cloud described in the poem is actually what the galaxy was like in the distant past! M83's appearance gives subtle clues to the processes happening within it.

Its stars are arranged in a spiral pattern, with a bar of stars spanning its centre. Astronomers think that bars like this funnel vast quantities of gas down to the centre of their guzzling galaxies, so that they can continue to form stars and emit light.

Interview with space scientist Rachel Cochrane

Thank you for writing the notes in this book! Can you tell us a bit about the work you do?

I study galaxies and how they evolve over time. I use data from large surveys to study the properties of galaxies, like how fast they are forming stars, how massive they are, and the environments they are in.

What made you want to be a space scientist?

I was eager to learn more about galaxy evolution and excited by the opportunities to observe at telescopes in unusual places. As part of my PhD I travelled to La Palma to observe galaxies on the William Herschel Telescope.

How can I get involved in astrophysics?

You can contribute to astrophysics research with any level of experience with 'citizen science'. Try www.zooniverse.org for some space-themed projects.

What's your favourite space fact?

Even though Andromeda is our closest neighbouring galaxy, the light we receive from it was emitted before humans like us existed on Earth!

Finally, what's your favourite poem in *Watcher of the Skies*?

'Recipe for Cosmic Cup Cakes' (page 14) is my favourite poem. Usually scientists try to break things down to understand them, but this poem mixes everything up into a fantastical dessert.

Rachel grew up in London but has now crossed the border to study for a PhD in Astrophysics in Edinburgh.

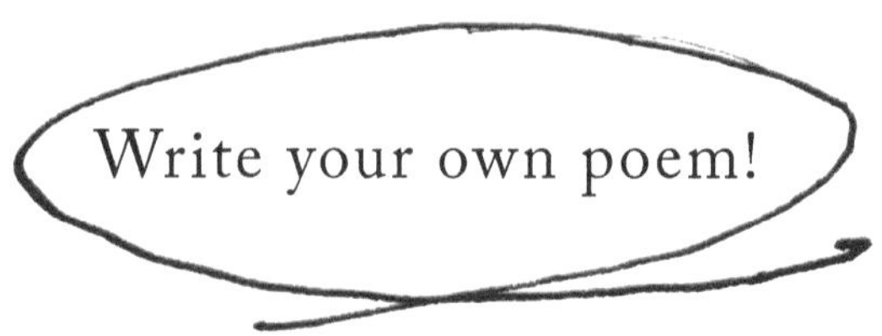

Fancy writing your own poem and maybe illustrating it afterwards? *Watcher of the Skies* editor Rachel Piercey has come up with some ideas to get you started.

In 'Recipe for Cosmic Cup Cakes' (page 14), Julie Anna Douglas throws various aspects of space into the mixing bowl. **Write your own cosmic recipe** for another kind of food, for example Star Stew or Moon Muffins. Try to include some relevant ingredients – so if it's Star Stew, you might have hydrogen, helium and mouldy old light.

Where will you serve your food, on what, and to whom? Let your imagination run riot!

Space scientist Rachel Cochrane tells us that the light from the Andromeda galaxy has been travelling for 2.5 million years to reach our eyes. **Write a poem called 'Song of Old Light'**, describing what the light has seen along its journey (feel free to mix fact with fiction), and how it feels to reach our human eyes.

In 'Message for Rosetta' (page 35), the Rosetta probe contains a disk etched with 1000 different languages. It would need a lot of coincidences for any aliens out there to find and be able to read these words, but it's a hopeful start!

Imagine you are stocking a capsule to send into space on a search for alien life. What would you include in this capsule to represent life on Earth? Will you focus on items associated with your particular home or country, or the whole world, or a mixture of both? Will the items all be physical objects or might you include some abstract ones, such as feelings and characteristics? Jot down some ideas, then choose your favourites to create your poem.

In his poem 'The Way Planets Talk' (page 54), Dom Conlon imagines how the characteristics of the planets influence the way they 'speak'. Sarah Doyle does this specifically for the planet Uranus in her poem 'Uranus: Roll Up, Roll Up' (page 84).

Choose a planet to research and then write a poem in its voice. First of all, write down the key characteristics of your planet (size, temperature, what it's made of etc) and then note down ideas for how your language could reflect each of these characteristics. For example, Venus is the hottest planet, so you might use lots of words which create the sensation of boiling heat. Jupiter spins fastest on its axis, so you could try creating a dizzying effect – but it's also the biggest planet and named after the Roman king of the gods, so you might use some regal language too.

Use your notes to write your poem, thinking carefully about how to order the details for the best effect.

About the editors

Rachel Piercey is a poet and editor for adults and children. She regularly performs her poems and runs writing workshops at schools and festivals across the country. Rachel co-edits the Emma Press books alongside Emma, who is one of her best friends from secondary school. Rachel's poems have appeared in *The Rialto, Magma, Poems in Which, Butcher's Dog* and *The Poetry Review*, as well as various Emma Press pamphlets and anthologies, and in 2008 she won the Newdigate Prize. She lives in London.

Emma Wright runs the Emma Press. After studying Classics at Brasenose College, Oxford, she did various odd jobs and ended up working in ebook production at Orion Publishing Group. She left in 2012 to follow her dreams and start a small publishing house. She lives in Birmingham.

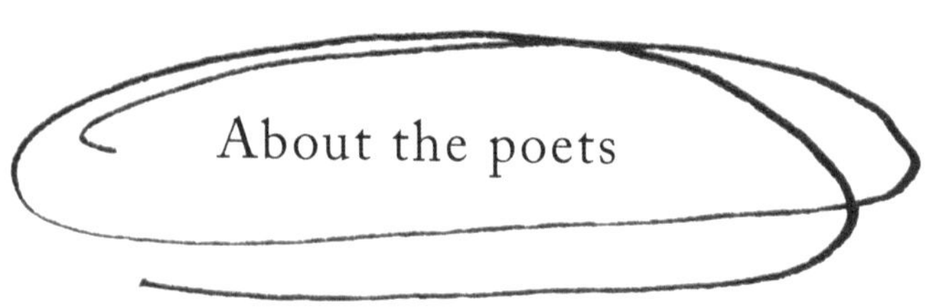

About the poets

Sohini Basak will never forget the time her brother woke her up at dawn to show the International Space Station orbiting over their hometown. She studied literature and creative writing at the universities of Delhi, Warwick and East Anglia, where she was awarded the Malcolm Bradbury continuation grant for poetry.

John Canfield grew up in Cornwall and now tries not to be a grown up in London. He writes poems and sometimes people put them in books and sometimes they don't. A promising career as a clown was scuppered by his desire to grow a beard.

Mary Anne Clark is reading English at Merton College, Oxford, and won the Newdigate Prize in 2016. Her poems have appeared in *The Mays*, *Oxford Poetry*, *Ash* and *Flight*, an anthology responding to the refugee crisis. She also has a poem in the Emma Press's *Falling Out of the Sky*.

Mandy Coe is the author of eight books and works regularly with schools and universities through author's visits. Her poetry has been published on the Poetry Archive, the *Guardian*, *Radio Times* and BBC television and radio. Her most recent collections are *There Will be Cherries* (Shoestring Press, 2016) and *If You Could See Laughter* (Salt, 2010).

Rebecca Colby taught English in Taiwan, worked for a Russian comedian and travelled the world as a tour director before she started writing books and poems for children. Her books include

There was a Wee Lassie who Swallowed a Midgie (2014), *It's Raining Bats & Frogs* (2015) and *Motor Goose*, coming out in 2017.

Dom Conlon is a children's writer, poet and space biscuit. His work regularly appears in *Stew Magazine* and alongside The Funeverse poets.

Dharmavadana's poems and short stories have appeared in many magazines. He has been a member of the Triratna Buddhist Order since 2005 and is poetry editor of the Buddhist arts magazine, *Urthona*. He has been working on a novel about Mars for three years and hopes to finish it eventually.

Julie Anna Douglas lives on the west coast of Scotland with her husband, son and daughter. Her poetry has appeared in *Spider* and *Ember* magazines in the USA, *The Caterpillar* in Ireland and various anthologies. She was shortlisted in 2015 for the National Literacy Trust/Bloomsbury Children's Books Poetry Prize and is a writer for *Amazing! Children's Educational Magazine*.

Sarah Doyle is the Pre-Raphaelite Society's poet-in-residence. She has been published in numerous journals and anthologies, placed in many competitions, and is co-author of *Dreaming Spheres: Poems of the Solar System* (PS Publishing, 2014). Sarah is currently studying for a Creative Writing MA at Royal Holloway. More at: www.sarahdoyle.co.uk

Inua Ellams was born in Nigeria and is an award-winning poet, playwright and founder of the Midnight Run. Identity, displacement and destiny are reoccurring themes in his work, in which he tries mixing the old with the new, the traditional with the contemporary. His books are published by Flipped Eye, Akashic and Oberon.

David Harmer has written many collections of children's poems as well as having other poems and stories published all over the place. He was a headteacher but he's lots better now and has spent many years working in schools getting everybody to write poems and laugh.

Philip Monks has published the pamphlets *Wake Up!*, *Nursery Verse* and *Wrap Yourself Up* and co-edited the poetry anthology *Iris Of A Peeping Eye.* He performs regularly and has run many poetry projects. He is a Visiting Lecturer in Creative Writing at Newman University and the University of Birmingham.

Cheryl Moskowitz is poet-in-residence at Highfield, a large multicultural north London primary school with over 48 languages spoken. Publications and broadcasts include *Poetry Pie* (CBeebies), *Can It Be About Me?* (Frances Lincoln), *A Life in the Year of... Poetry at Highfield* and *The Girl is Smiling* (Circle Time Press).

Dale Neal lives in the village of Barrowford in Lancashire. When not cutting hair he can be found writing about monkeys, monsters and bouncy castles. His first book, *Hippo in a Half Pipe*, is due for release in early 2017.

Rachael M Nicholas was born in Birmingham in 1987. Her work has appeared in *Magma, Gigantic Sequins, The Cadaverine* magazine and *Banshee.* In 2012 she won an Eric Gregory Award. Her first pamphlet, *Somewhere Near in the Dark*, was published by Eyewear Publishing in 2014.

Richard O'Brien's poems for children were published in *Falling Out of the Sky* by the Emma Press in 2015. He has since seen them reimagined in drawings and performed back to him as choreographed dance routines. In 2015, he took part in the Myths and Monsters poetry tour, and now does author visits for the charity Pop Up Projects. Richard has never been to space, but he did once nearly fall asleep in the San Francisco Planetarium.

Suzanne Olivante lives in Sussex and writes poetry and jokes for children. Her work has been placed in competitions and published in anthologies. She was placed second in the Plough Prize Poem for Children in 2010 and was a finalist for the National Literacy Trust Poetry Prize in 2015.

Abigail Parry spent seven years as a toymaker, before completing her PhD in play and games in contemporary poetry. She can most commonly be found writing about beguiling animals, unhappy monsters, magic and mischief. She received an Eric Gregory Award in 2010.

Gita Ralleigh has completed her MA in Creative Writing at Birkbeck College, University of London and published stories in Wasafiri and the Bellevue Literary Review. She is working on a novel for children, a steampunk fantasy set in India in which mechanical elephants feature.

Robert Schechter has published in *Highlights for Children, National Geographic Book of Nature Poems, The Washington Post, Anon, Leviathan Quarterly* and elsewhere. He lives on Long Island, New York.

Lawrence Schimel was born in New York and has lived in Madrid, Spain, for over 17 years. He won the Rhysling Award from the Science Fiction Poetry Association in 2002. His poems are anthologized in *The Random House Treasury of Light Verse,* Neil Gaiman's *The Sandman: The Book of Dreams*, and *Slow Things* (Emma Press, 2015).

Mike Sims studied English at Oxford University. He co-founded Forest Poets and works for The Poetry Society. 'Alien Boy' is inspired by Michael Ondaatje's wonderful novel, *The Cat's Table* (Vintage, 2012).

Camellia Stafford was born in Warwickshire and she read English Literature and Language at King's College London. Her debut pamphlet, *another pretty colour, another break for air*, is published by tall-lighthouse and *Letters to the Sky*, her first collection, is published by Salt. Camellia lives in Warwickshire and works in museum education.

Jon Stone is one half of Sidekick Books, who publish collaborative anthologies of poetry on the subject of computer games, animals, dinosaurs and more. He is a survivor of the Lego Ice Planet Wars and an infamously terrible A-wing pilot.

Kate Wakeling lives in Oxford. When not writing poems, she works as an ethnomusicologist at Trinity Laban Conservatoire of Music & Dance and writer-in-residence with Aurora Orchestra. A pamphlet of her poetry (*The Rainbow Faults*) is published by The Rialto and a collection of poetry for children aged 8+ (*Moon Juice*) has just been published by the Emma Press.

Rob Walton is a writer and performer of poetry for children and adults, as well as short stories, scripts and flash fiction. He won the 2015 NFFD micro-fiction award and his poems have been published by the Emma Press (*Slow Things*), Butcher's Dog and others. His children's poems were published in *Let's Play!* (Frances Lincoln).

Kate Wise fits poetry around two under-fives and a career in law. She has been published in various magazines in print and online, most recently in *Structo* and *Poems in Which*. Her work appeared in two Emma Press anthologies in 2015.

The Emma Press

small press, big dreams

The Emma Press is a Birmingham-based publishing house which makes poetry books for adults and children. Emma Wright set it up in 2012 and works on all the books with her best friend from school, Rachel Piercey.

Emma Press books are starting to win prizes, including the Poetry Book Society Pamphlet Choice Award and the Saboteur Award for Best Collaborative Work. The Emma Press has also been shortlisted for the Michael Marks Award for Poetry Pamphlet Publishers twice (2014 and 2015).

Falling Out of the Sky. Poems about Myths and Monsters, the first Emma Press poetry book for children, was published in 2015 and was shortlisted for CLiPPA, the CLPE poetry book award. The next Emma Press anthology for children, coming out in 2017, will be themed around kings and queens...

You can find out more about the Emma Press and buy books directly from us here:
http://theemmapress.com

Also from the Emma Press

Falling Out of the Sky

Poems about Myths and Monsters

Edited by Rachel Piercey and Emma Wright

An Emma Press Children's Anthology (aimed at 9+)

RRP £8.50 / ISBN 978-1-910139-18-9

Who helped Theseus defeat the Minotaur? How did Antaboga the serpent create the world? Why was Arachne turned into a spider? And what did Loki do to bring about the end of the world? Find out in *Falling Out of the Sky*, a treasury of poems about myths and legends by twenty modern poets. Featuring mischievous gods, ferocious villains, witches, wizards and monsters – who might not all be as monstrous as the stories say...

Also from the Emma Press

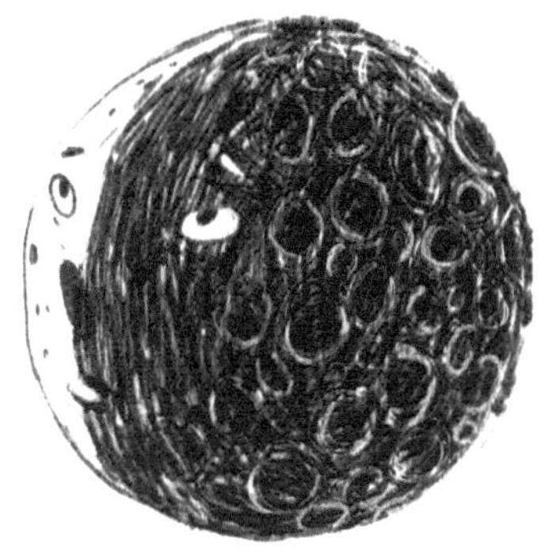

Moon Juice

Poems by Kate Wakeling

With illustrations by Elīna Brasliņa

An Emma Press Children's Collection (aimed at 8+)

RRP £8.50 / ISBN 978-1-910139-49-3

Meet Skig, who's meant to be a warrior (but is really more of a worrier). Meet a giddy comet, skidding across the sky with her tail on fire. Put a marvellous new machine in your pocket and maybe you'll be able to fix all your life's problems. Kate Wakeling's first book of poems for children is full of curious characters and strange situations. The poems she writes are always musical, sometimes magical, and full of wonder at the weirdness of the world.

www.ingramcontent.com/pod-product-compliance
Ingram Content Group UK Ltd.
Pitfield, Milton Keynes, MK11 3LW, UK
UKHW041957190726
13854UKWH00005B/2023

9 781910 139431